THE NEW GUITAR TAB
BIG BOOK
'70s & '80s

I'M ALRIGHT

TRUCKIN' ROSANNA

SMOKE FROM A DISTANT FIRE

PARANOID PLAY THAT FUNKY MUSIC

THUNDER ROAD DANCING QUEEN

THIS MASQUERADE INTO THE NIGHT

SATURDAY IN THE PARK D'YER MAK'ER

20TH CENTURY BOY DO YOU FEEL LIKE WE DO

BLINDED BY THE LIGHT LIMELIGHT ONLY WOMEN BLEED

BAD TO THE BONE LIVE AND LET DIE

WHAT A FOOL BELIEVES GO YOUR OWN WAY

25 OR 6 TO 4 HOLD THE LINE LIGHTS

L.A. WOMAN BEHIND BLUE EYES

EUROPA (EARTH'S CRY HEAVEN'S SMILE)

FEELIN' STRONGER EVERY DAY LOLA LOWDOWN

WHATEVER GETS YOU THRU THE NIGHT

WELCOME TO MY NIGHTMARE DOWN ON IT

Produced by
Alfred Music
P.O. Box 10003
Van Nuys, CA 91410-0003
alfred.com

Printed in USA.

ISBN-10: 1-4706-1098-1
ISBN-13: 978-1-4706-1098-2

CONTENTS

ARTIST INDEX

20TH CENTURY BOY

Words and Music by
MARC BOLAN

8

Spoken: *My friends say it's fine, they say it's good,*
I don't believe it's like Robin Hood.
I'm like a car, I drive like a plane,
I wanna hang your head in the falling rain.
Ah, oh, yeah. Wow!

25 OR 6 TO 4

Words and Music by
ROBERT LAMM

Flash - ing lights_____ a - gainst_____ the sky,_____
Want - ing just_____ to stay_____ a - wake,_____
Search - ing for_____ some - thing_____ to say,_____

giv - ing up,_____ I close_____ my eyes._____
won - d'ring how_____ much I_____ break can take._____
wait - ing for_____ the break of day._____

Horns

twen-ty - five___ or six___ to four._____

*Chords are implied.

molto rit.

BAD TO THE BONE

Open G tuning:
⑥= D   ③= G
⑤= G   ②= B
④= D   ①= D

Words and Music by
GEORGE THOROGOOD

Moderately ♩ = 98
Intro:
G

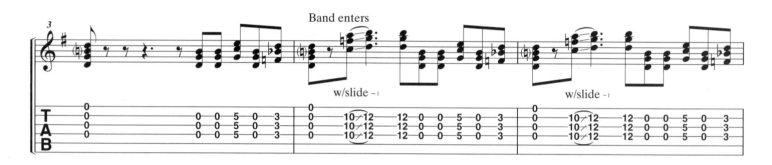

*Chord shapes are played with slide worn on pinky or with fingers 3 and 1.

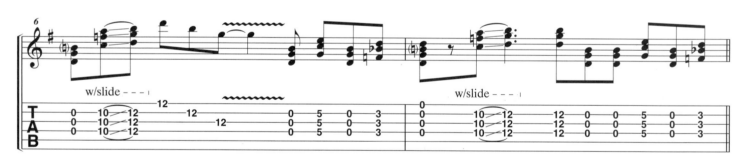

𝄋 *Verses 1, 2, & 4:*

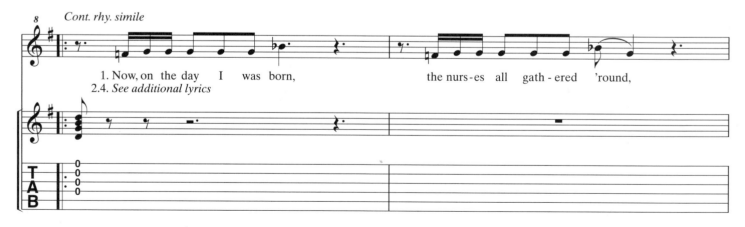

Bad to the Bone - 7 - 1

and they gazed in wide won - der   at the joy they have found.__

The head nurse spoke up,   said, "Leave this one a - lone."__

She could tell right a - way__   that I was bad to the bone.

1.

Bad__ to the bone.   Bad__ to the bone.

B - b - b - b - b - b - b - bad,__   b - b - b - b - b - b - b - bad.__

B - b - b - b - b - b - b - bad,__   bad__ to the bone.

2.3.

B - b - b - b - b - b - b - bad,__   b - b - b - b - b - b - b - bad.__

To Coda ⊕

B - b - b - b - b - b - b - bad,__   bad__ to the bone.

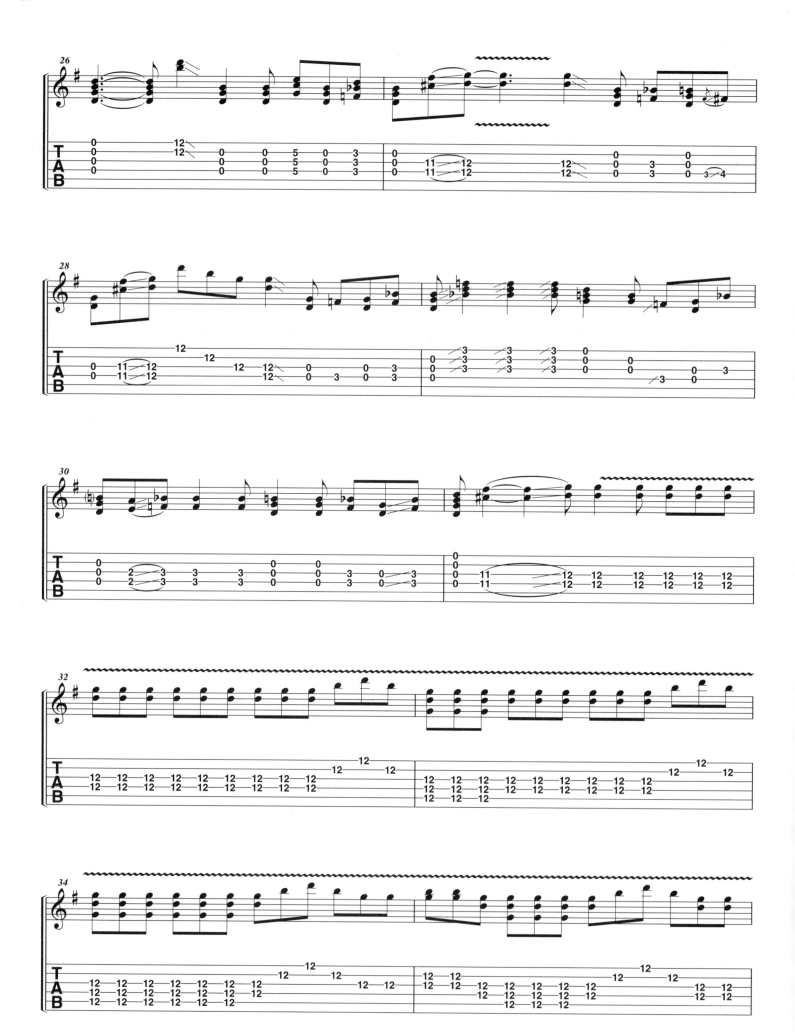

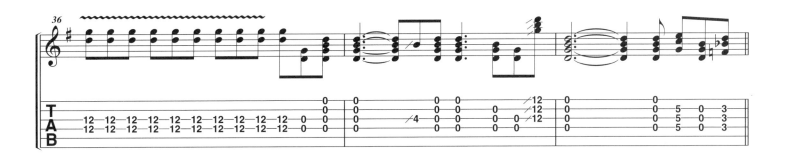

Verse 3:

Cont. rhy. simile

I'll make a rich wom-an beg,___ and I'll make a good wom-an steal.

I'll make an old wom-an blush, and I'll make a young girl squeal.

I wan-na be yours, pret-ty ba-by, yours and yours a - lone.___

I'm here to tell you, hon - ey, that I'm bad to the bone.

B - b - b - b - b - b - b - bad,___ b - b - b - b - b - b - b - bad.___

B - b - b - b - b - b - b - bad,___ bad to the bone.

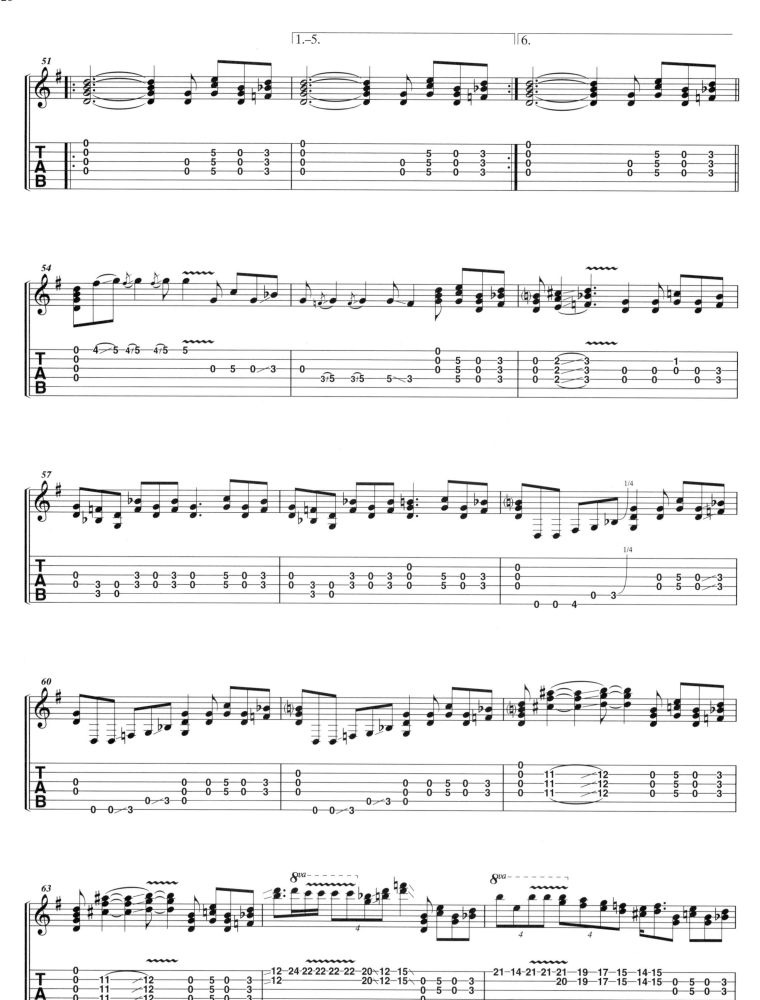

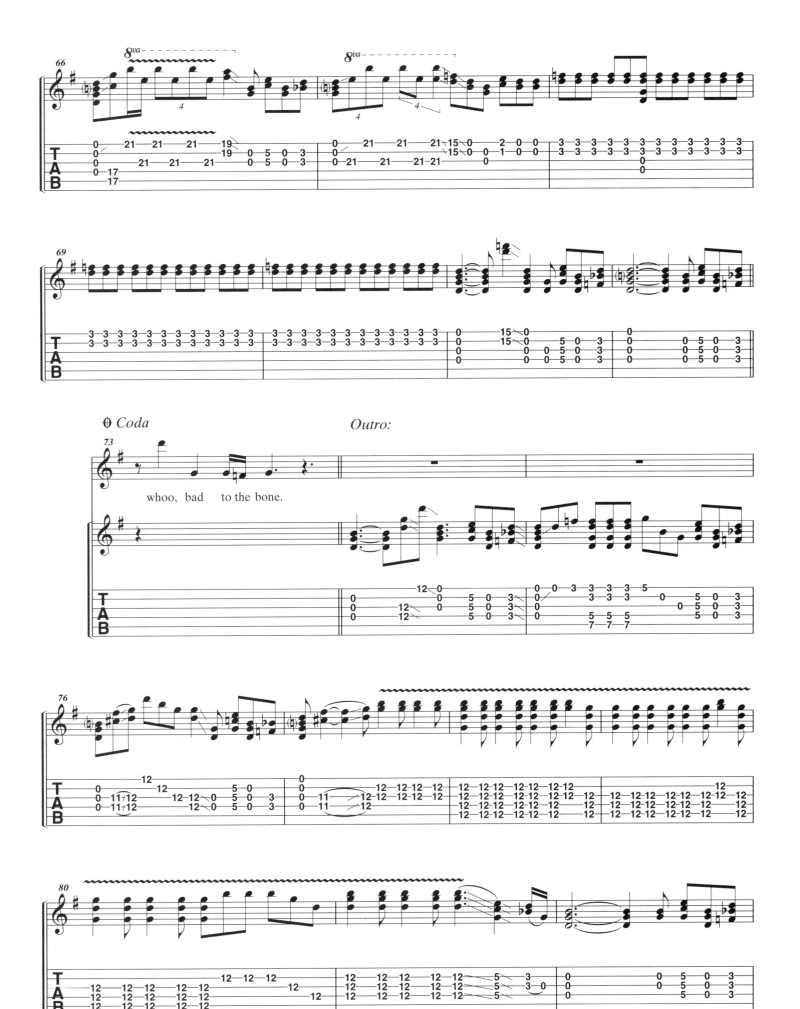

whoo, bad to the bone.

Bad to the Bone - 7 - 6

w/o slide

trem. pick

Verse 2:
I broke a thousand hearts
Before I met you.
I'll break a thousand more, baby,
Before I am through.
I wanna be yours, pretty baby,
Yours and yours alone.
I'm here to tell ya, honey,
That I'm bad to the bone,
Bad to the bone.
B-b-b-b-b-b-b bad,
B-b-b-b-b-b-b bad.
B-b-b-b-b-b-b bad,
Bad to the bone.
(To Guitar Solo 1:)

Verse 4:
Now, when I walk the streets,
Kings and Queens step aside.
Every woman I meet, heh, heh,
They all stay satisfied.
I wanna tell you, pretty baby,
What I see I make my own.
And I'm here to tell ya, honey,
That I'm bad to the bone,
Bad to the bone.
B-b-b-b-b-b-b bad,
B-b-b-b-b-b-b bad.
B-b-b-b-b-b-b bad,
Whoo, bad to the bone.
(To Outro:)

BEHIND BLUE EYES

Words and Music by
PETER TOWNSHEND

Behind Blue Eyes - 7 - 5

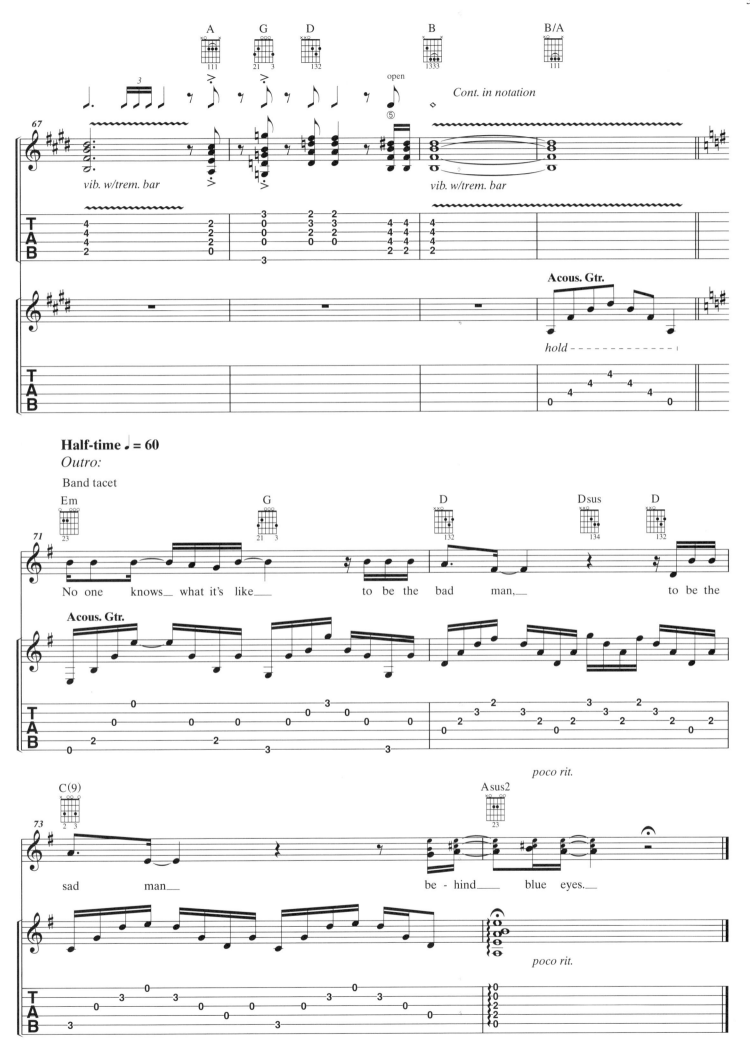

BLINDED BY THE LIGHT

Bright rock ♩ = 138

Words and Music by
BRUCE SPRINGSTEEN

*Bass plays C pedal tone throughout first chorus.

Blinded by the Light - 7 - 1

38

Instrumental:

Play 4 times

But, ma - ma,_____ that's where the fun___ is.___

(Inst. solo cont. behind vocal)   ...end solo)

Gtr.

Ma-ma al-ways told me not to look in - to the eyes of the sun._____ But, ma - ma,_____

Blinded by the Light - 7 - 5

that's where the fun is.

3. Some

revved up like a deuce, another runner in the night. Blind-

1. Mad-

-ed by the light,

revved up like a deuce, another

-man drummers, bummers, Indians in the summer with a teen-age dip-lo-mat.
with a sling-shot fi-n'lly found a tender spot and throws his lov-er in the sand.

runner in the night. Blind-ed by the light, revved up

In the dumps with the mumps as the ad-o-les-cent pumps his way
And some blood-shot for-get-me-not said, "Dad-dy's with-in ear-shot; save the

Blinded by the Light - 7 - 6

BROWN SUGAR

Words and Music by
MICK JAGGER and KEITH RICHARDS

Moderately ♩ = 126

Intro:

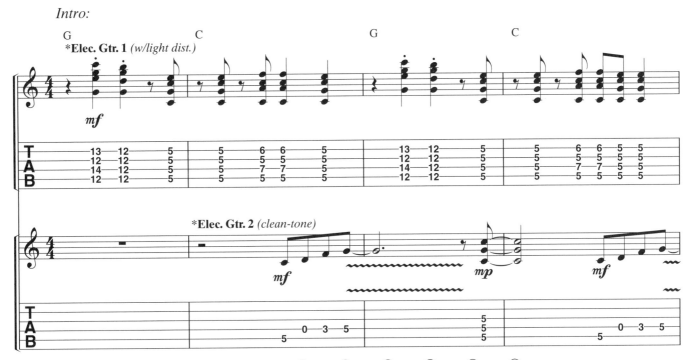

*Elec. Gtrs. 1 & 2 are both in Open G tuning: ⑥ = D; ⑤ = G; ④ = D; ③ = G; ② = B; ① = D

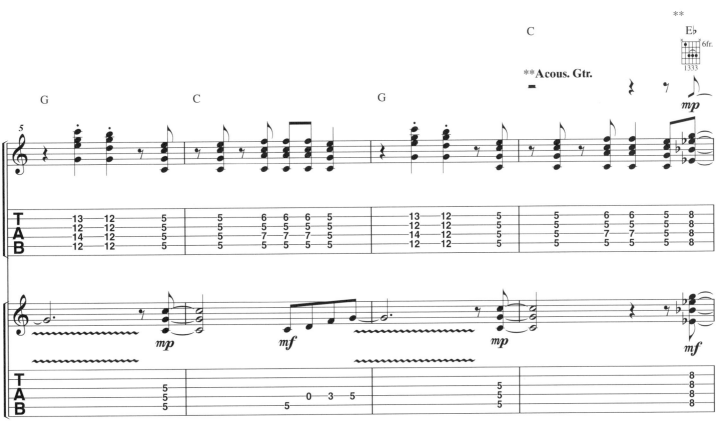

**Chord frames reflect Acous. Gtr. in standard tuning, entering at meas. 8.

Brown Sugar - 7 - 1

44

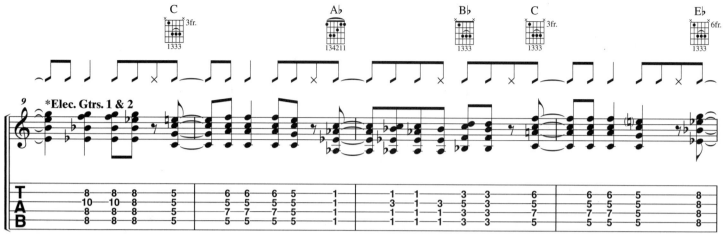

*Composite arrangement.

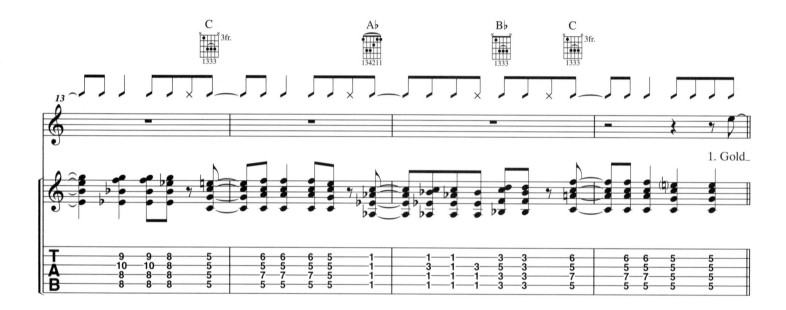

Verse 2:
Drums beating, cold English blood runs hot,
Lady of the house wondrin' where it's gonna stop.
House boy knows that he's doin' alright,
You should a heard him just around midnight.
(To Chorus:)

Verse 3:
I bet your mama was a tent show queen,
And all her boyfriends were sweet sixteen.
I'm no schoolboy but I know what I like,
You should have heard me just around midnight.
(To Chorus:)

CAN'T YOU SEE

Moderately slow ♩ = 84

Intro:

Words and Music by
TOY CALDWELL

1. Gon - na take a freight train   down at the sta - tion, Lord,__
2. *See additional lyrics*

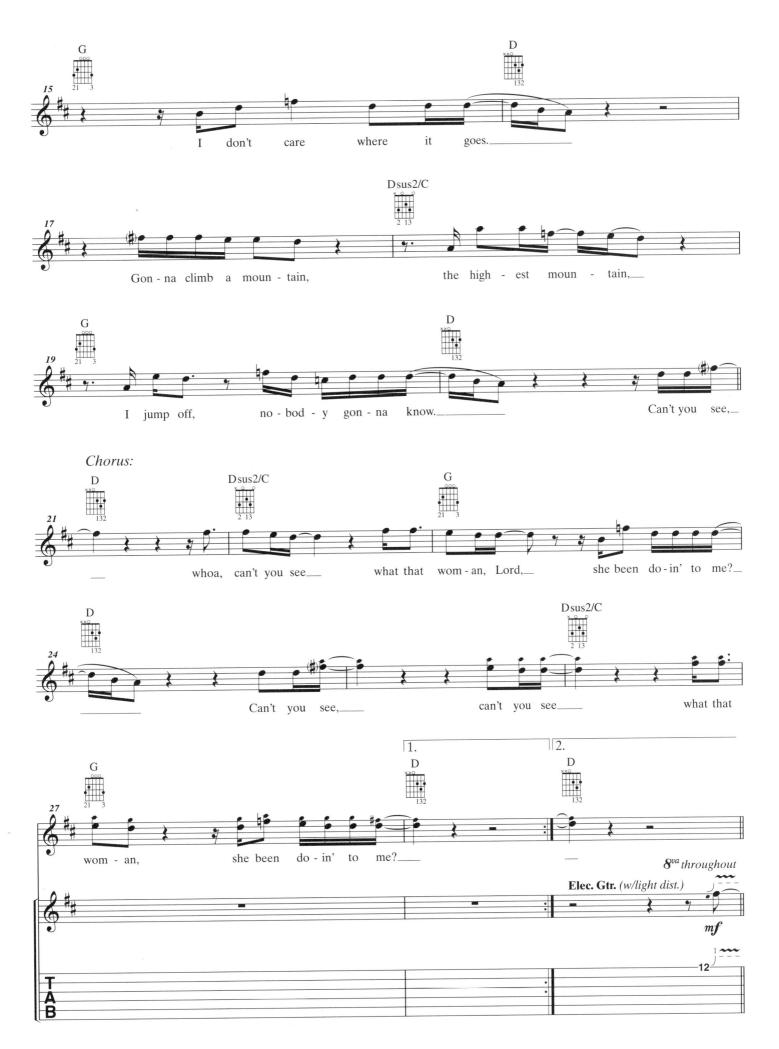

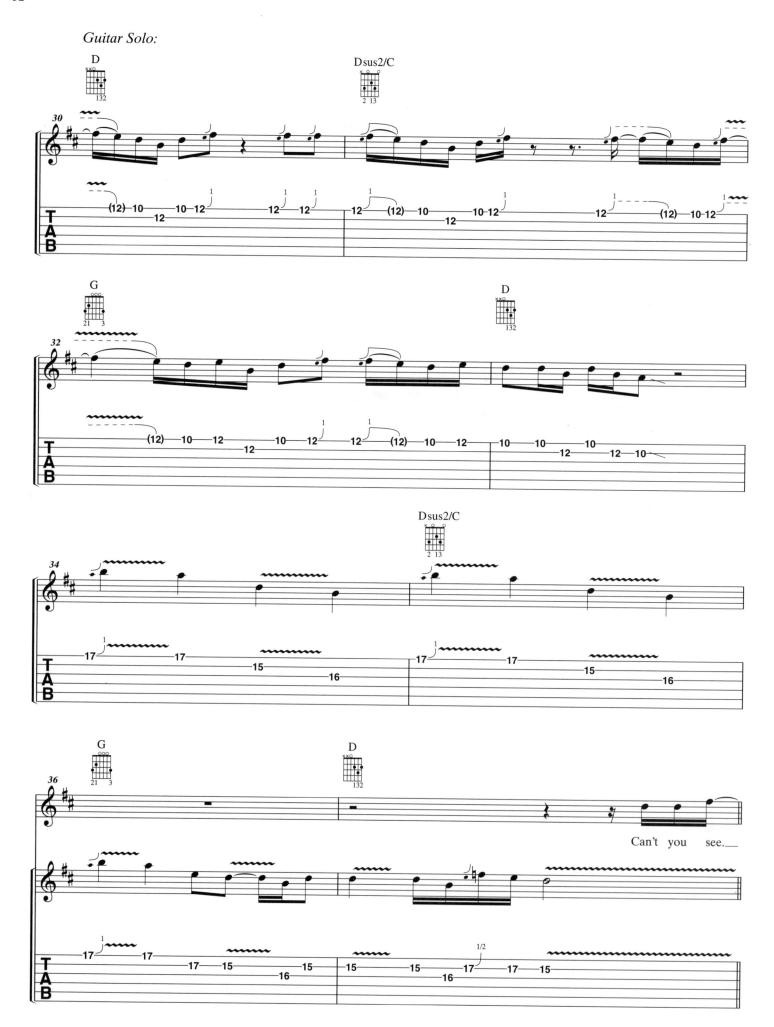

Guitar Solo:

Can't you see.___

Chorus:

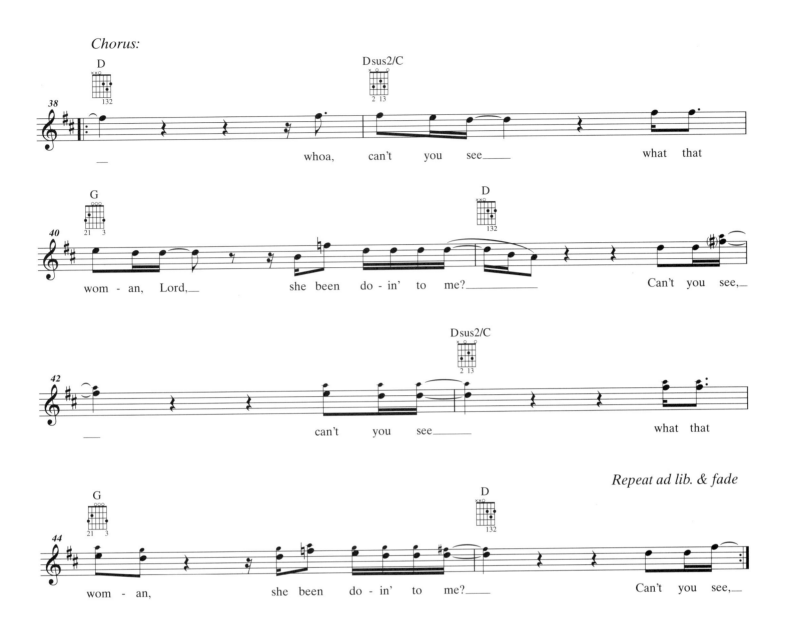

whoa, can't you see____ what that wom - an, Lord,____ she been do - in' to me?_____ Can't you see,____ can't you see____ what that wom - an, she been do - in' to me?____ Can't you see,____

Repeat ad lib. & fade

Verse 2:
I'm gonna buy a ticket now,
As far as I can, ain't never comin' back.
Grab me a southbound all the way to Georgia now,
'Til the train, it run out of track.
(To Chorus:)

D'YER MAK'ER

Note: The original recording sounds an eighth tone (25 cents) flat of concert pitch.
To play along, tune all strings slightly flat.

Words and Music by
JIMMY PAGE, JOHN BONHAM,
JOHN PAUL JONES, and ROBERT PLANT

Guitar Solo: (Note: This solo looks more complicated than it really is. Before trying to play it on guitar, sing the solo along with the recording to get familiar with its melodic aspects.)

D.S. ℅ al Coda

Coda

Repeat ad lib. and fade

DANCING QUEEN

Words and Music by
BENNY ANDERSSON, STIG ANDERSON
and BJORN ULVAEUS

Dancing Queen - 3 - 1

58

Dancing Queen - 3 - 2

DON'T STOP BELIEVIN'

Words and Music by
JONATHAN CAIN, NEAL SCHON
and STEVE PERRY

Interlude:

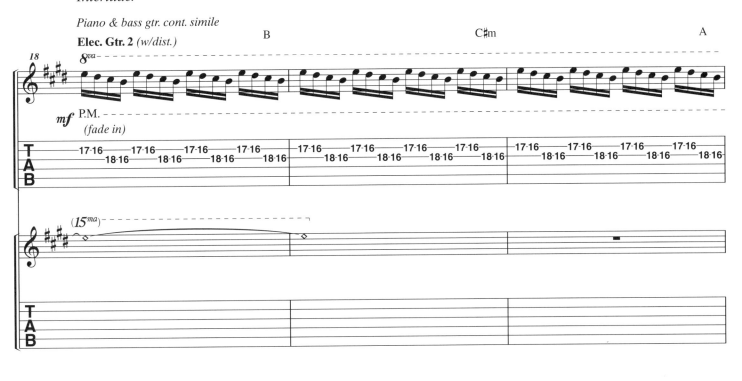

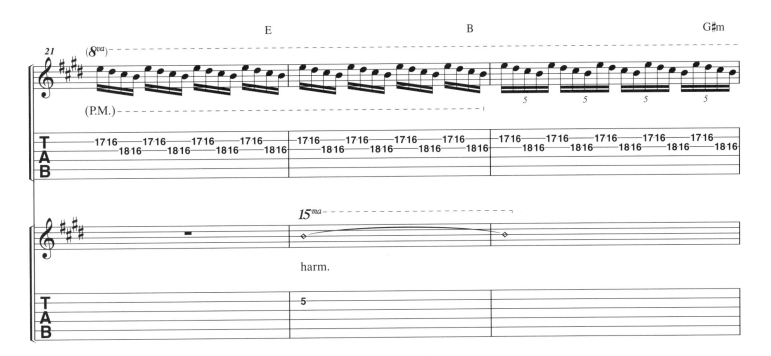

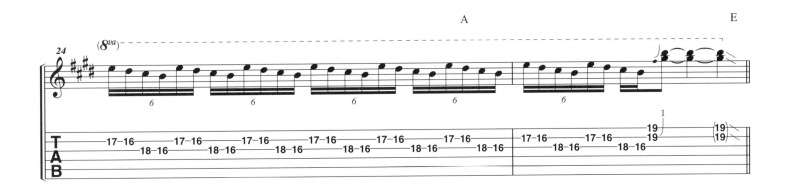

Verse 3:

Elec. Gtrs. 1 & 2 tacet

A sing-er in a smok-y room.__ The smell of wine and cheap per - fume.___

For a smile_ they can share the night;_ it goes on and on__ and on__ and on.___

℁ *Bridge:*

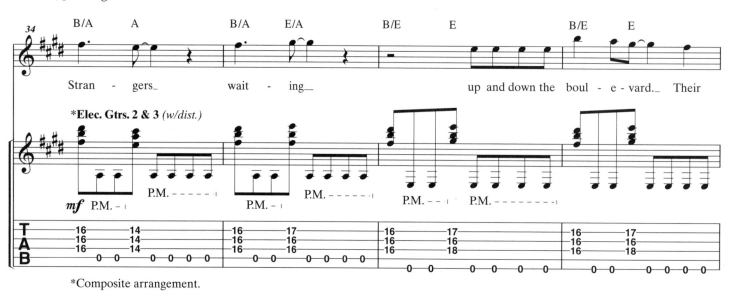

Stran - gers_ wait - ing_ up and down the boul - e - vard.__ Their

*Elec. Gtrs. 2 & 3 *(w/dist.)

*Composite arrangement.

shad - ows_ search - ing__ in the night._____

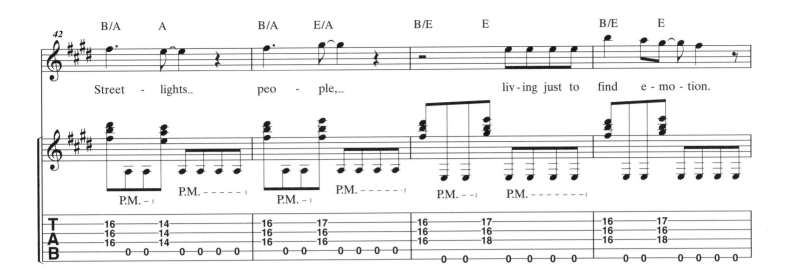

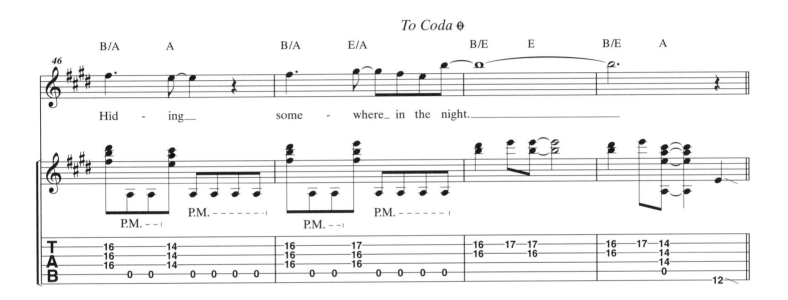

Interlude:

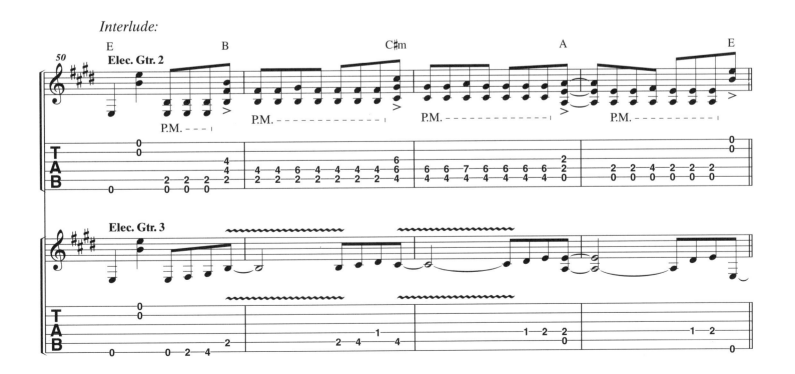

Verse 4:

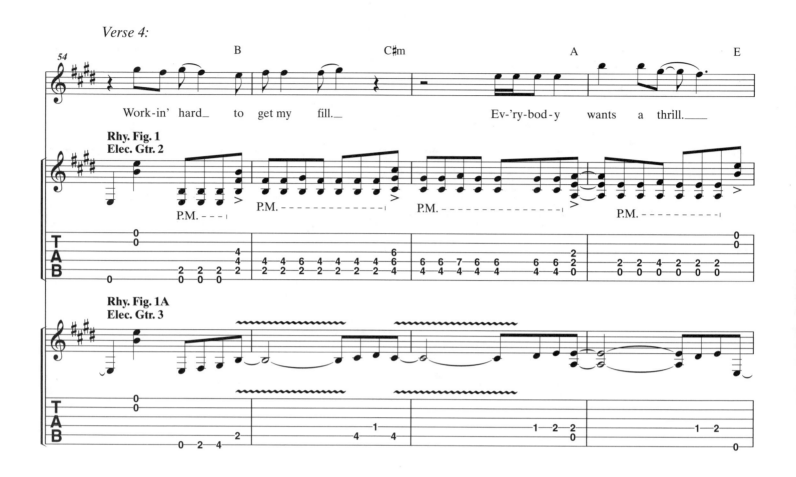

Work-in' hard___ to get my fill.___ Ev-'ry-bod-y wants a thrill.___

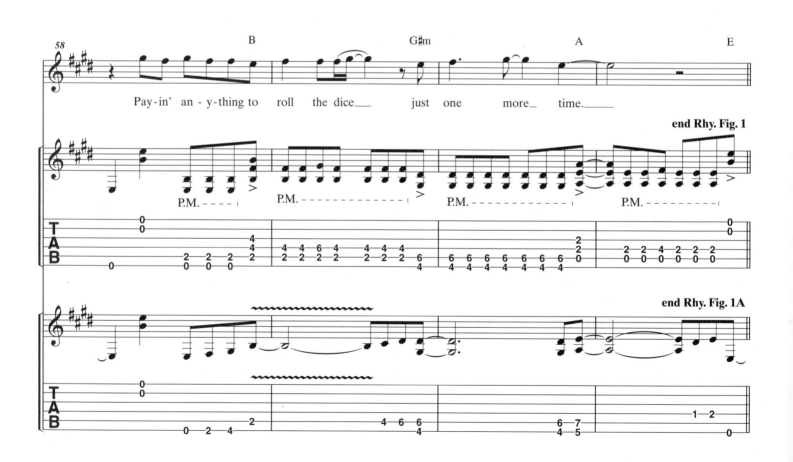

Pay-in' an-y-thing to roll the dice___ just one more___ time.___

Verse 5:

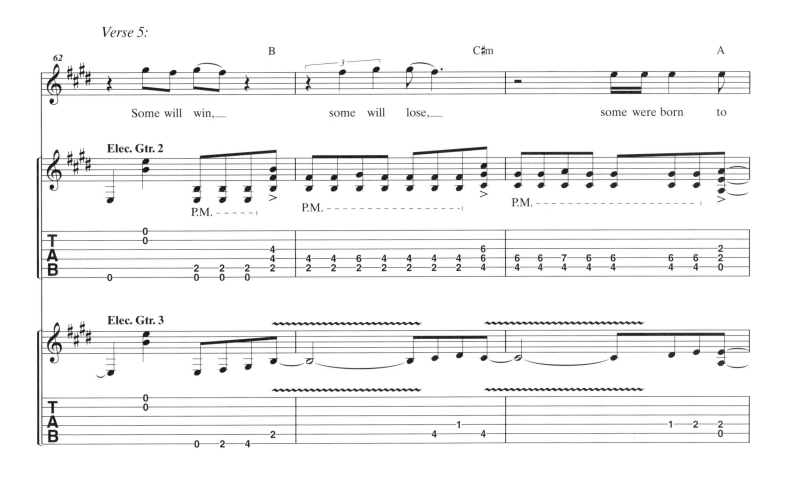

Chorus:
w/Rhy. Figs. 1 (Elec. Gtr. 3) & 1A (Elec. Gtr. 4) both 3 times

Don't_ stop be - liev - in', hold on to the feel - in'.

Street_ lights peo - ple!____

Don't_ stop be - liev - in'. Hold on!____

Street_ lights peo - ple!____

Begin fade

Don't_ stop be - liev - in', hold on__ to that feel - ing.____

Fade out

Street_ lights peo - ple!____

DO YOU FEEL LIKE WE DO

(live—radio edit)

Words and Music by
PETER FRAMPTON, JOHN SIOMOS,
RICK WILLIS and MICK GALLAGHER

Moderately ♩ = 106

Intro:

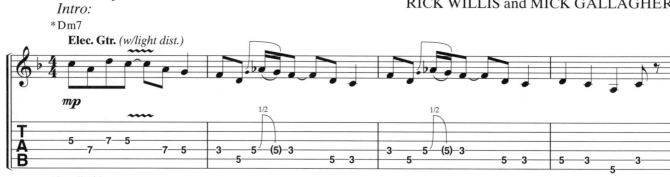

*Implied harmony.

Do You Feel Like We Do - 9 - 1

*Implied harmony.

*Fm7

F G

Verse:

A

E

1.Well, woke up this morn-ing with a wine glass in my hand.___
2. My friend got bust-ed just the oth-er day. They said,

A

Whose___ wine, what___ wine, where the hell did I dine?___
"Don't___ walk, don't___ walk, don't walk a - way."___

Do You Feel Like We Do - 9 - 2

70

Do You Feel Like We Do - 9 - 4

Do You Feel Like We Do - 9 - 6

*Implied harmony.

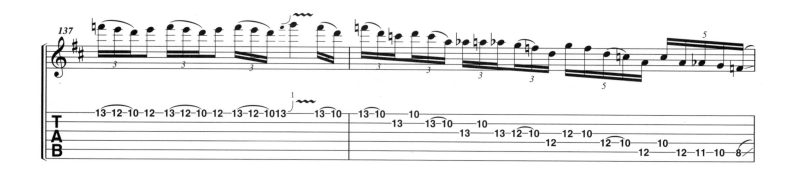

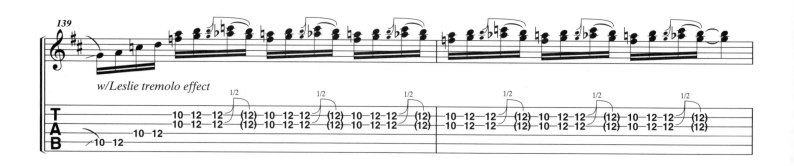

Fmaj7

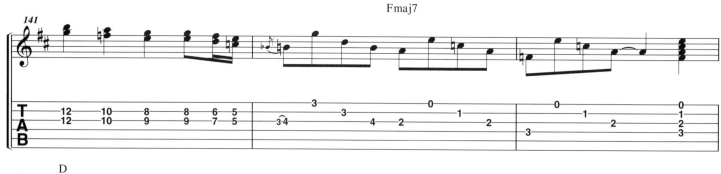

D

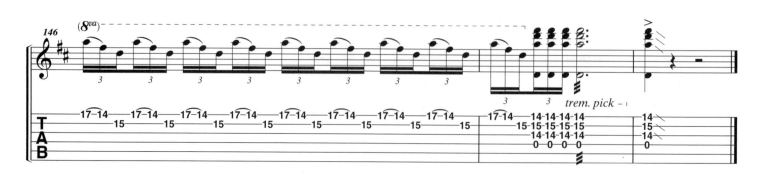

EUROPA (EARTH'S CRY HEAVEN'S SMILE)

Music by
CARLOS SANTANA and TOM COSTER

Europa (Earth's Cry Heaven's Smile) - 7 - 1

Europa (Earth's Cry Heaven's Smile) - 7 - 3

Europa (Earth's Cry Heaven's Smile) - 7 - 5

Europa (Earth's Cry Heaven's Smile) - 7 - 6

Europa (Earth's Cry Heaven's Smile) - 7 - 7

FEELIN' STRONGER EVERY DAY

Words and Music by
PETER CETERA and JAMES PANKOW

Feelin' Stronger Every Day - 4 - 1

86

Feelin' Stronger Every Day - 4 - 3

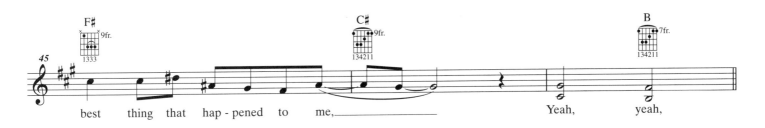

best thing that hap-pened to me,_____ Yeah, yeah,

Outro:

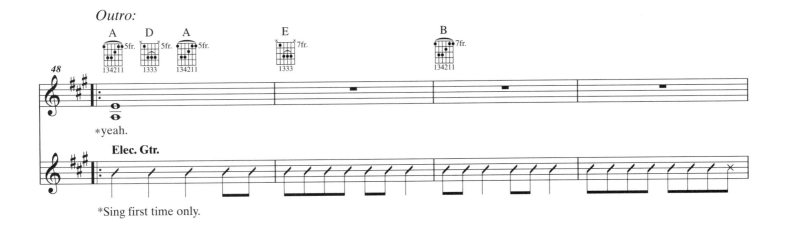

*yeah.

Elec. Gtr.

*Sing first time only.

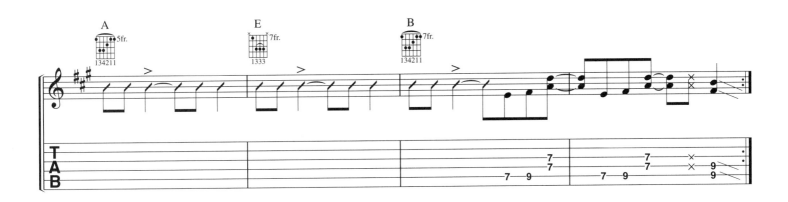

Chorus:

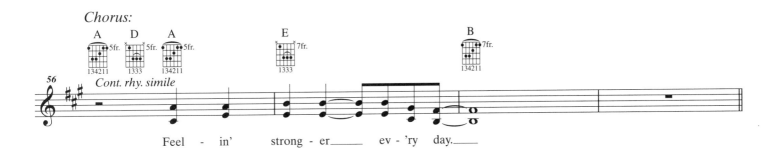

Cont. rhy. simile

Feel - in' strong - er_____ ev - 'ry day._____

Repeat and fade

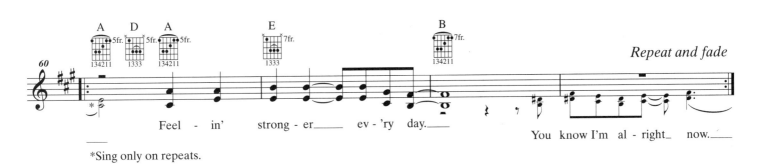

Feel - in' strong - er_____ ev - 'ry day._____

You know I'm al - right_ now._____

*Sing only on repeats.

Feelin' Stronger Every Day - 4 - 4

GO YOUR OWN WAY

Capo III → D   A   G   Bm

Frames for Acous. Gtr. w/capo III.

Words and Music by
LINDSEY BUCKINGHAM

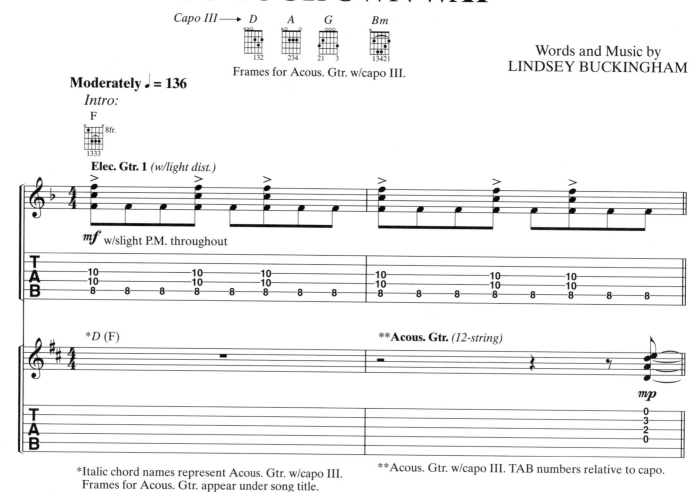

*Italic chord names represent Acous. Gtr. w/capo III.
Frames for Acous. Gtr. appear under song title.

**Acous. Gtr. w/capo III. TAB numbers relative to capo.

Go Your Own Way - 4 - 2

You can go___ your own_ way,_____ go___ your own_ way. ___ your own_ way.

Guitar Solo:

Elec. Gtr. 1 & Acous. Gtr. resume verse fig. simile

Elec. Gtr. 2 *(w/dist.)*

Chorus:

Elec. Gtr. 1 & Acous. Gtr. resume chorus fig. simile

You can go___ your own_ way,_____ go___ your own_ way._____

HOLD YOUR HEAD UP

Words and Music by
ROD ARGENT and CHRIS WHITE

*Chords implied by organ.

Play 6 times

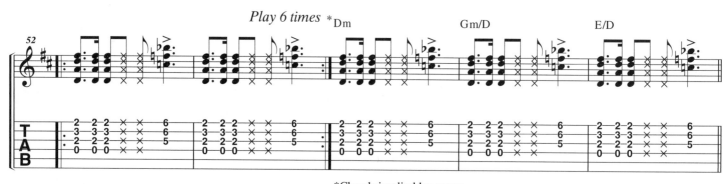

*Chords implied by organ.

*Elec. Gtr. makes random noises with slide bar, quickly rubbing across the first three strings, starting at the end of the fingerboard and slowly descending towards the nut.

Bass Gtr. & Elec Gtr. cont. simile

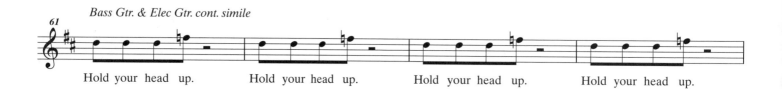

Hold your head up.   Hold your head up.   Hold your head up.   Hold your head up.

HOLD THE LINE

Words and Music by
DAVID PAICH

Moderately ♩. = 98

Intro:

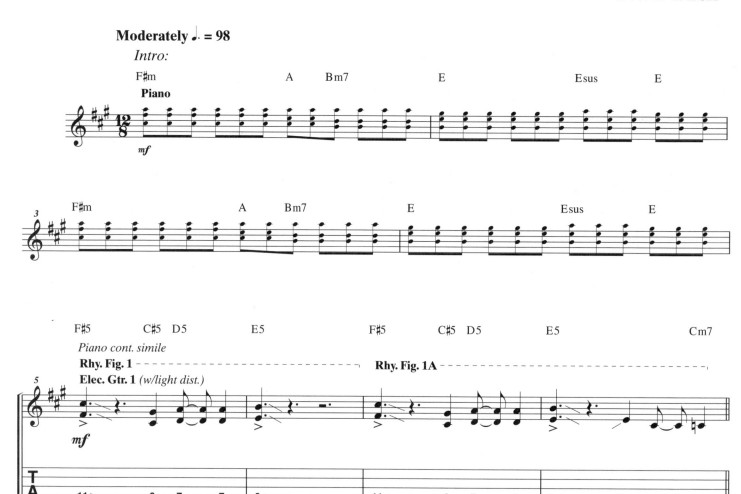

% *Verse:*

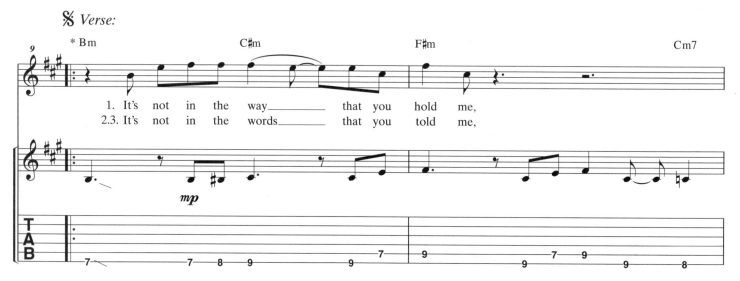

*Chords implied by keybds.

98

Hold the Line - 7 - 3

Guitar Solo:
w/Rhy. Fig. 1 *(Elec. Gtr. 1) 7 times, simile (see meas. 5–6)*

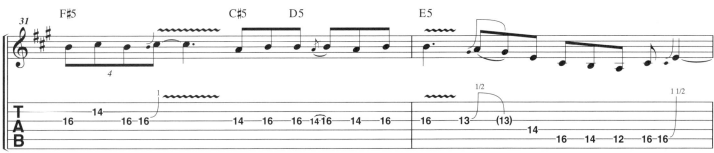

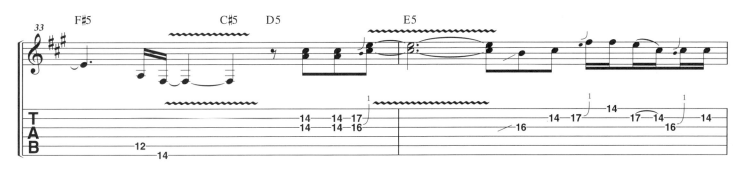

Hold the Line - 7 - 4

w/Rhy. Fig. 1A (Elec. Gtr. 1), simile (see meas. 7–8)

D.S. % al Coda

102

Hold the Line - 7 - 7

I'M ALRIGHT

(from *CADDYSHACK*)

Words and Music by
KENNY LOGGINS

*Elec. Gtr. 1 in Drop D tuning:
⑥ = D ③ = G
⑤ = A ② = B
④ = D ① = E

Moderately in 2 ♩ = 82
Chorus:

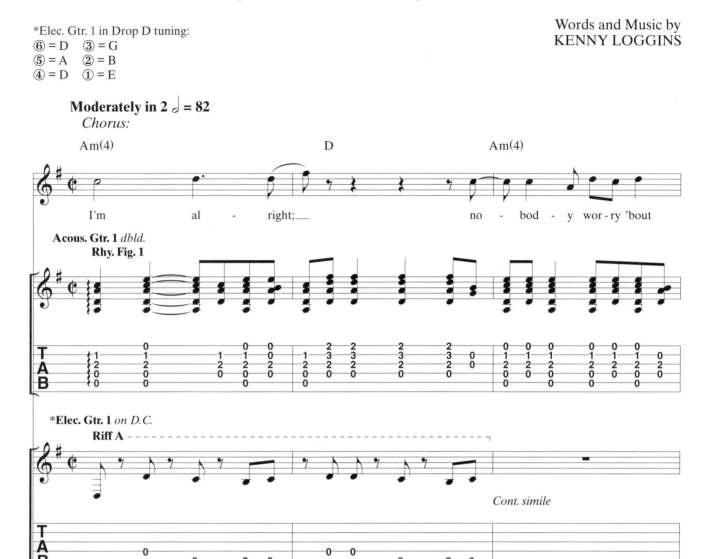

I'm Alright - 5 - 1

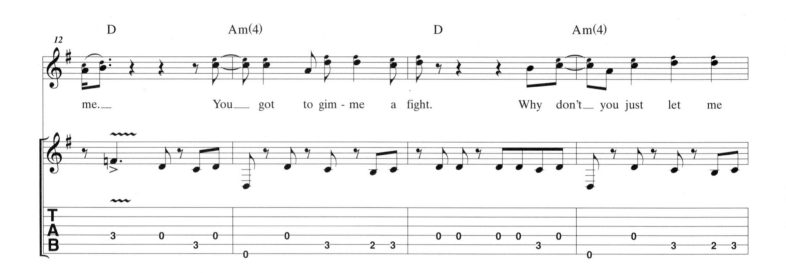

Verse:

-in',_____ own_____ heart_____ beat - in',_____ own_____ heart_____ beat-

Pre-chorus:

-in'._____ Own_____ heart._____ Yeah._____ "Got - ta
Don't it

catch you lat - er."_____ "No,_____ no, can - non - ball it right a - way."_____
get you mov - in'? M - m - m - m - man, it makes me feel good._____

Get it up and get you a job._____

Some_____ Cin - der - el - la kid._____

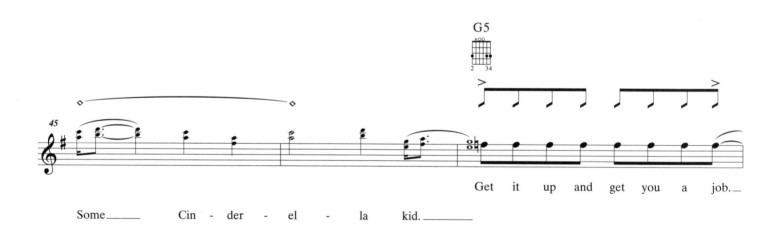

Duh, duh, duh, duh, duh, duh, duh, duh. Duh, duh, duh, duh, duh, duh, duh, duh. Boom, boom, boom.
I'm.

I'm Alright - 5 - 4

Outro Chorus:

w/Rhy. Fig. 1 *(Acous. Gtr. 1) 4 times, simile*

w/Riff A *(Elec. Gtr. 1) 8 times, simile*

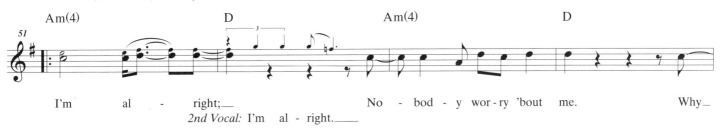

I'm al - right;___ No - bod - y wor - ry 'bout me. Why___

2nd Vocal: I'm al - right.___

___ you got to gim - me a fight?___ Can't___ you just let it be?___

___ I'm al - right;___ don't___

I'm al - right;___

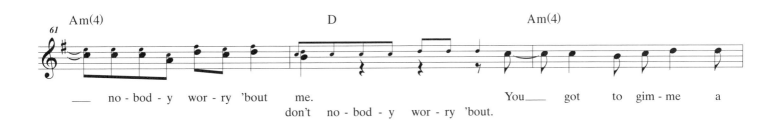

___ no - bod - y wor - ry 'bout me. You___ got to gim - me a

don't no - bod - y wor - ry 'bout.

Repeat ad lib. to fade

fight?___ Why don't___ you just let me be?

Why you wan - na fight? Don't you let___ me.___

I'm Alright - 5 - 5

IMAGINE

Words and Music by
JOHN LENNON

Slowly ♩ = 75

Intro:

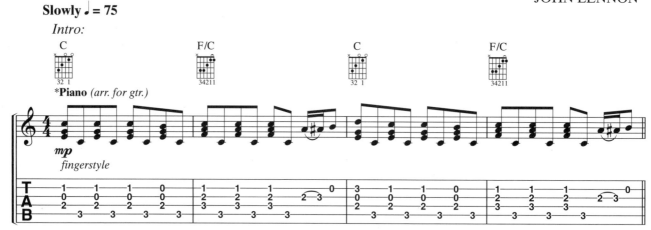

*Piano *(arr. for gtr.)*

mp

fingerstyle

*There is no guitar on the original recording.

Verse:

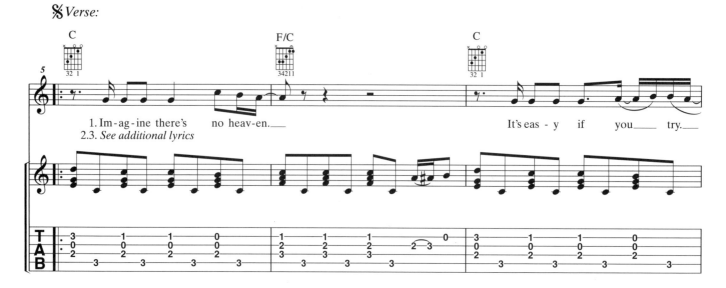

1. Im-ag-ine there's   no heav-en.___ It's eas-y   if   you___   try.___
2.3. *See additional lyrics*

___   No   hell___   be-low us,___

Imagine - 3 - 1

I hope some-day_____ you'll join us_____

and the world_____ will be as one._____

rit.

and the world_____ will live as one._____

D.S. %

Verse 2:
Imagine there's no countries,
It isn't hard to do.
Nothing to kill or die for
And no religion too.

Pre-chorus 2:
Imagine all the people
Living life in peace.
You...
(To Chorus:)

Verse 3:
Imagine no possessions,
I wonder if you can.
No need for greed or hunger,
A brotherhood of man.

Pre-chorus 3:
Imagine all the people
Sharing all the world.
You...
(To Chorus:)

IN THE DARK

Words and Music by
BILLY SQUIRE

Moderately ♩ = 116

Intro:

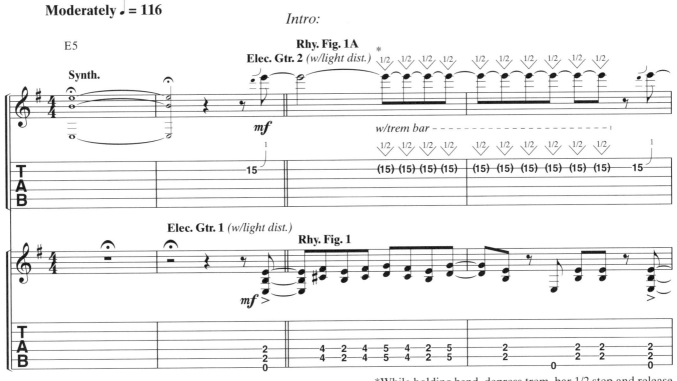

*While holding bend, depress trem. bar 1/2 step and release
in an 1/8th note rhythm pattern.

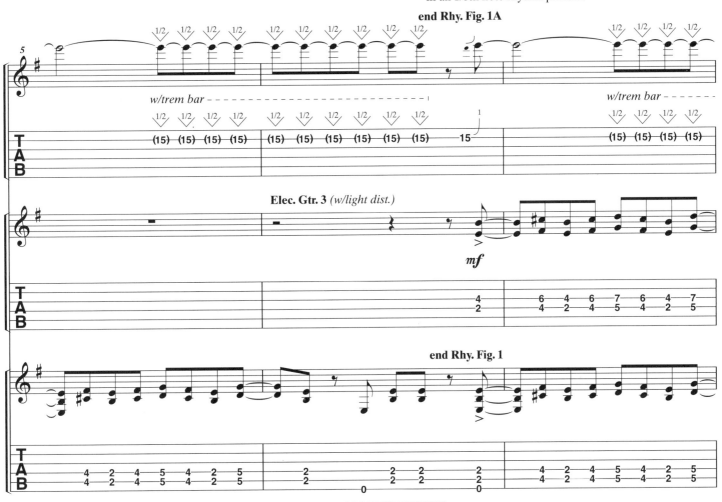

In the Dark - 7 - 1

𝄉 Verse:

1. Life is - n't eas - y from the sin - gu - lar side,___ down in the hole, some e -
2. You nev - er lis - ten to the voic - es in - side,___ they fill your ears as you
3. You take no in - t'rest, no o - pin - ion's too dear,___ you make the rounds, oh, you

Rhy. Fig. 2
Elec. Gtr. 1

w/slight P.M. -

*Elec. Gtr. 2 fill simile on repeats.

In the Dark - 7 - 3

Pre-chorus:

need____ a friend,_____ would you tell____ no lies.____ Would you
break____ a - way_____ from your al - i - bis.____ Can you
face____ the fire_____ when you see____ me there.____ Can you

take____ me in,_____ are you lone - ly in the dark.____
make____ a play,_____ will you meet me in the dark.____
feel____ the fire,_____ will you love me in the dark.____

Chorus:

In the dark.____

Elec. Gtr. 3

In the dark.

Elec. Gtr. 1

w/slight P.M. -

Guitar Solo:
w/Rhy. Fig. 2 (Elec. Gtr. 1), simile (see meas. 11–16)

In the Dark - 7 - 7

INTO THE NIGHT

Words and Music by
ROBERT TEPPER and BENNY MARDONES

Moderately slow ♩ = 86

L.A. WOMAN

Words and Music by
THE DOORS

Verse 1:

just got in - to town a-bout an hour a - go.___

I

took a look a-round, see which___ way the wind___ blows.

With a lit - tle girl in a Hol-ly-wood bun - ga - low.___

Are you a

luck-y lit - tle la - dy in the cit - y of light?___

Or just an -

L.A. Woman - 16 - 2

1.–3.   4.

Interlude 1:

Elec. Gtrs. 1 & 2

I

Bridge 1:

see your hair is burn - ing;____

hills are filled with fire._____   If they

say I nev-er loved____ you,_   you

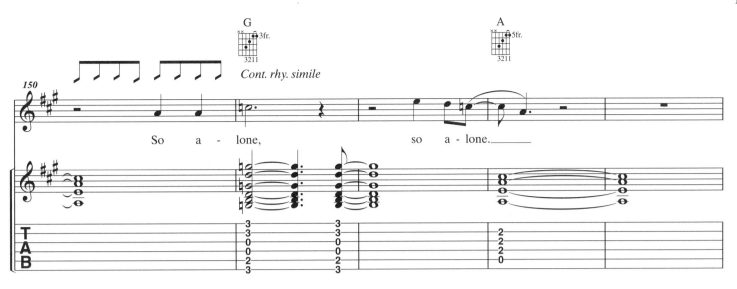

So a - lone, so a - lone.____

Mo - tel mon-ey, mur - der mad - ness,

a-change the mood from glad____ to sad - ness.

Half time ♩ = 80

Elec. Gtr. 2 tacet

Bridge 2:

keep on ris - in'._____ Mis-ter Mo - jo___ ris - in'._____ Mis-ter

Mo - jo ris - in'._____ Mo - jo ris - in'._____ Got my

Mo - jo ris - in'._____ Mis-ter Mo - jo ris - in'._____ Got-ta

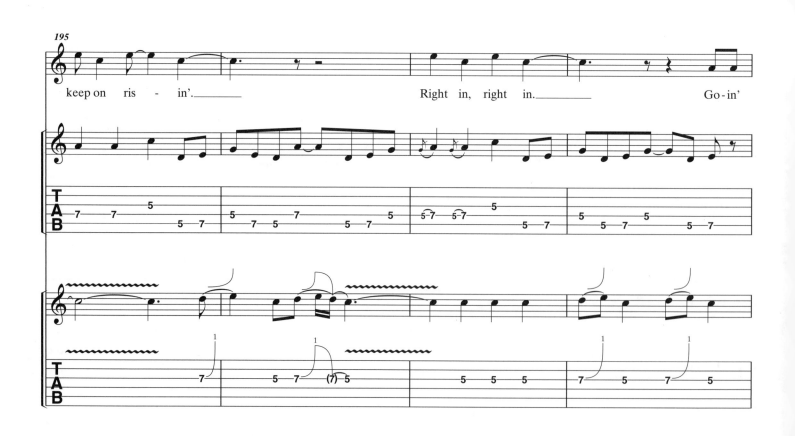

keep on ris - in'._____ Right in, right in._____ Go-in'

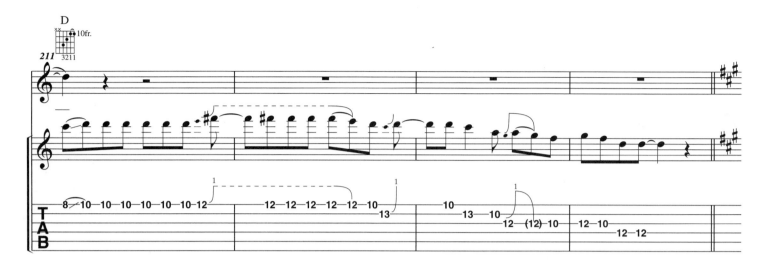

Verse 2:

L. A. Wom-an._____ You're my wom-an._____ My lit-tle

L. A. Wom-an._____ Yeah, my L. A. Wom-an._____

Ay! Ay! Come on, come on, L. A. Wom-an, come on.

LIGHTS

Words and Music by
NEAL SCHON and STEVE PERRY

Moderately slow ♩. = 69

Intro:

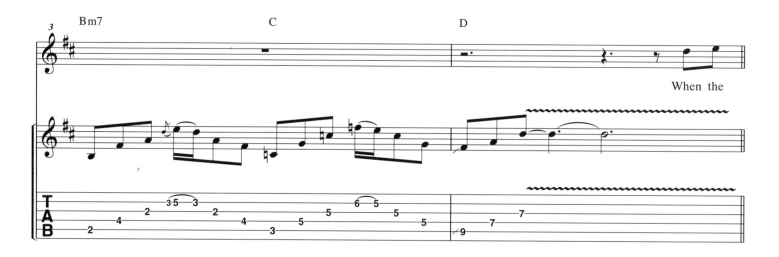

Chorus:

Lights - 7 - 1

Chorus:

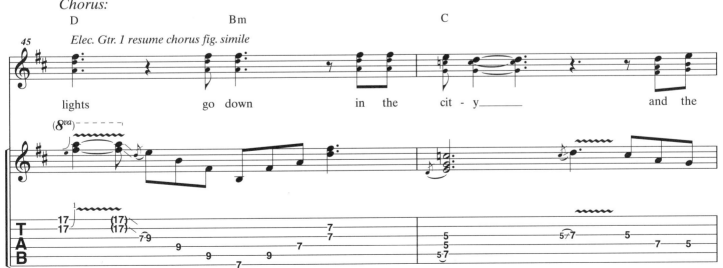

144

Lights - 7 - 7

LIMELIGHT

Words by NEIL PEART
Music by GEDDY LEE and ALEX LIFESON

Limelight - 7 - 1

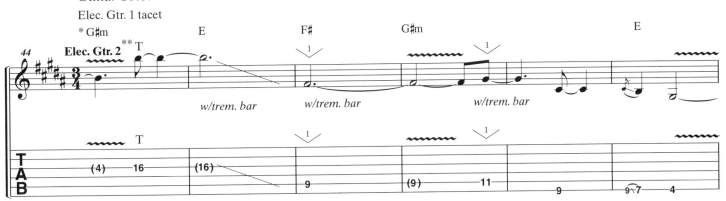

*Chords are implied by Bass Gtr.
**While holding B note, tap high B note (fret 16) with right-hand index finger,
then gradually depress trem. bar w/left hand.

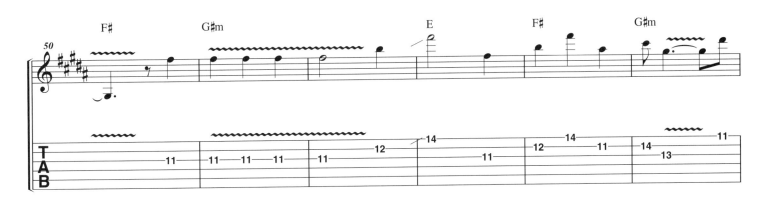

*Strike string while trem. bar is depressed
and then release bar to normal position.

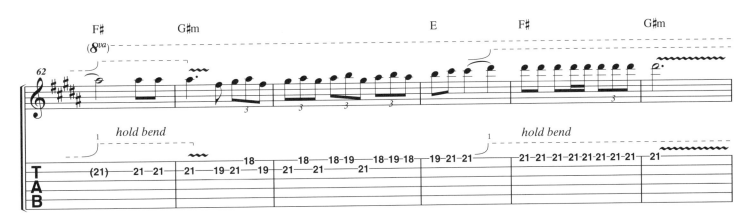

Limelight - 7 - 5

Limelight - 7 - 7

LOLA

Words and Music by
RAY DAVIES

LOVE, REIGN O'ER ME

*Elec. Gtrs. 1 & 2 tuned down 1/2 step:

⑥ = E♭   ③ = G♭
⑤ = A♭   ② = B♭
④ = D♭   ① = E♭

**Words and Music by
PETER TOWNSHEND**

**Acous. Gtr. in standard tuning w/Capo I:

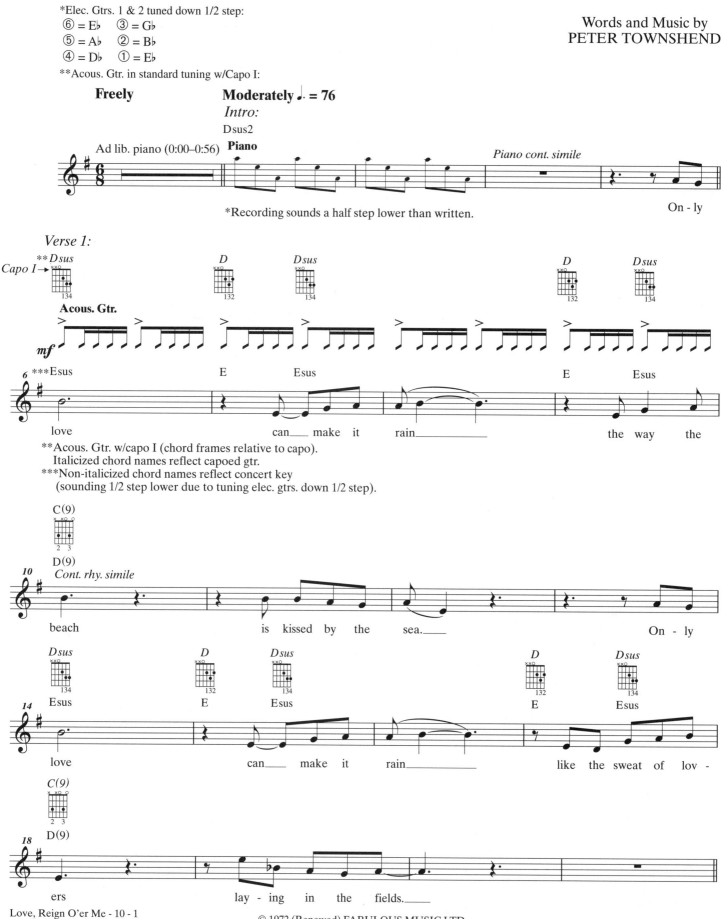

Love, Reign O'er Me - 10 - 1

Chorus:

158

Love, Reign O'er Me - 10 - 4

Love, Reign O'er Me - 10 - 5

162

Love, Reign O'er Me - 10 - 8

Love, Reign O'er Me - 10 - 9

Love, Reign O'er Me - 10 - 10

LOWDOWN

Words and Music by
BOZ SCAGGS and DAVID PAICH

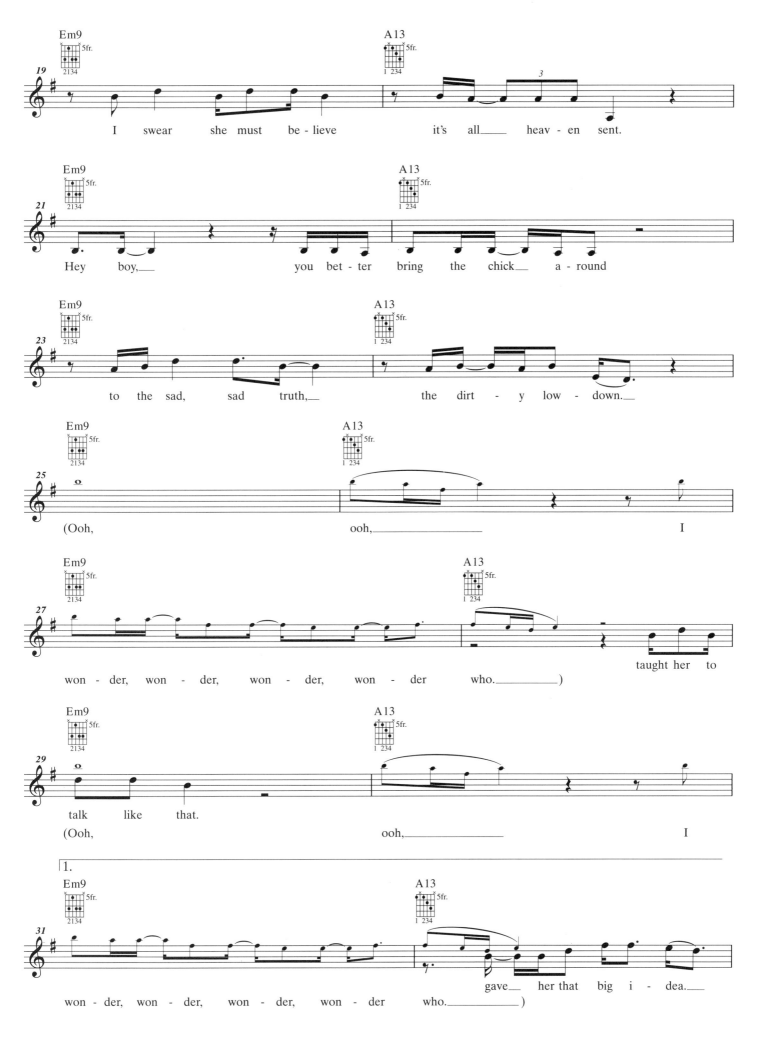

168

Come on back down to earth, son, dig the low, low, low, low, low - down.

*Chord frames are for reference.
**Elec. Gtr. 2 simile 2nd time.

Elec. Gtr. 1 resume intro fig. simile (see meas. 5–8)

Interlude:

To Coda ⊕

*Chords implied by keybd.

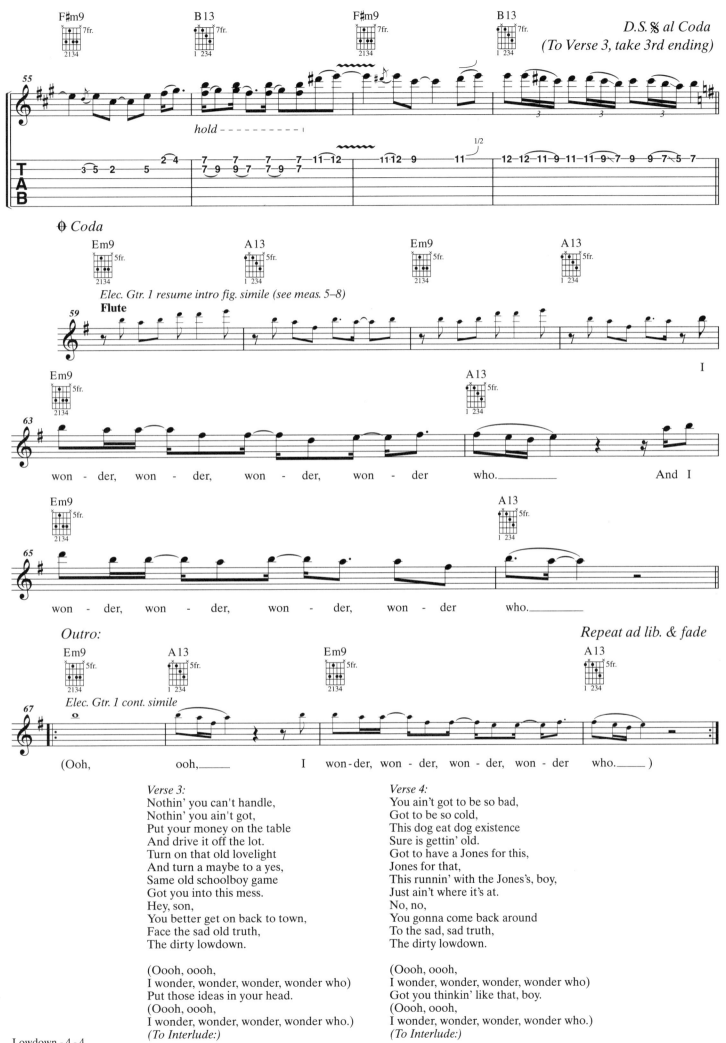

Verse 3:
Nothin' you can't handle,
Nothin' you ain't got,
Put your money on the table
And drive it off the lot.
Turn on that old lovelight
And turn a maybe to a yes,
Same old schoolboy game
Got you into this mess.
Hey, son,
You better get on back to town,
Face the sad old truth,
The dirty lowdown.

(Oooh, oooh,
I wonder, wonder, wonder, wonder who)
Put those ideas in your head.
(Oooh, oooh,
I wonder, wonder, wonder, wonder who.)
(To Interlude:)

Verse 4:
You ain't got to be so bad,
Got to be so cold,
This dog eat dog existence
Sure is gettin' old.
Got to have a Jones for this,
Jones for that,
This runnin' with the Jones's, boy,
Just ain't where it's at.
No, no,
You gonna come back around
To the sad, sad truth,
The dirty lowdown.

(Oooh, oooh,
I wonder, wonder, wonder, wonder who)
Got you thinkin' like that, boy.
(Oooh, oooh,
I wonder, wonder, wonder, wonder who.)
(To Interlude:)

LIVE AND LET DIE

Words and Music by
PAUL McCARTNEY and
LINDA McCARTNEY

Live and Let Die - 3 - 1

MONEY

Words and Music by
ROGER WATERS

Guitar Solo:

Outro:

B5

Repeat ad lib. and fade
w/ad lib. Gtr. fills
(use guitar solo as a model for improv.)

PARANOID

Words and Music by
ANTHONY IOMMI, JOHN OSBOURNE,
WILLIAM WARD and TERENCE BUTLER

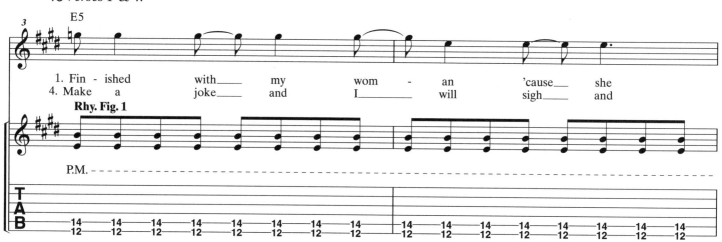

Paranoid - 4 - 1

Oh,_____ yeah.__

Interlude:
w/Rhy. Fig. 1 *(Elec. Gtr.)*

Verse 3:
w/Rhy. Fig. 1 *(Elec. Gtr.)*

I need some - one to_____ show me__ the things in life__ that I can't find.

I can't see__ the things__ that make_ true hap - pi - ness,__ I must be blind.

Guitar Solo:

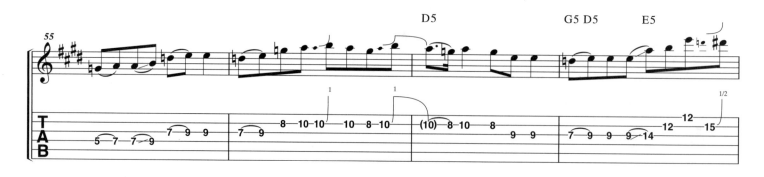

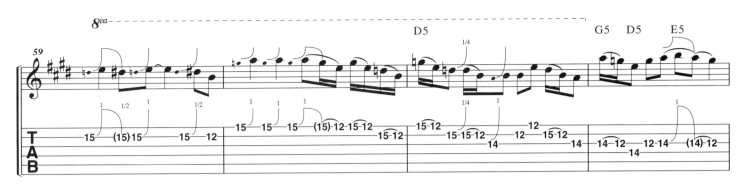

Interlude:

w/Rhy. Fig. 1 *(Elec. Gtr.)*

D.S. % al Coda

Coda   *Outro:*

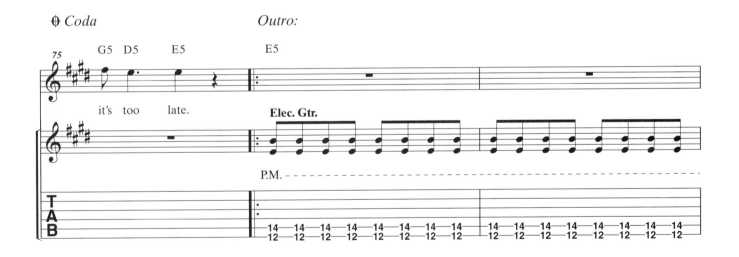

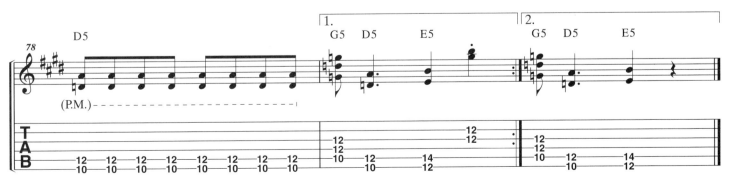

PLAY THAT FUNKY MUSIC

Words and Music by
ROBERT PARISSI

Play That Funky Music - 6 - 1

190

Play That Funky Music - 6 - 3

ROSANNA

Words and Music by
DAVID PAICH

*Chord frames are for reference throughout except on the pre-chorus.

1. All I wan-na do when I wake up in the morn-ing is see your eyes,___
2. I can see your face still shin-ing through the win-dow on the oth-er side,___

Ros - an - na,___ Ros - an - na,___ nev - er thought that a
Ros - an - na,___ Ros - an - na,___ I did - n't know that a

*While holding 15th fret bend play 16th fret,
then 15th fret, and then gradually release bend.

202

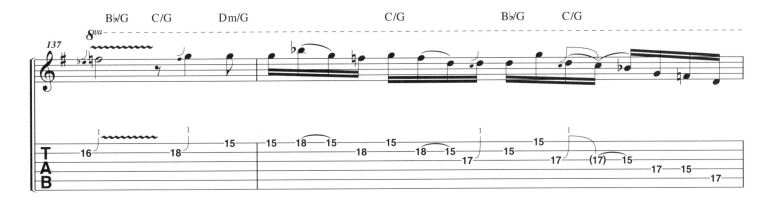

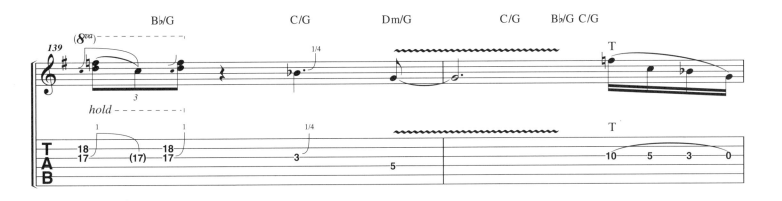

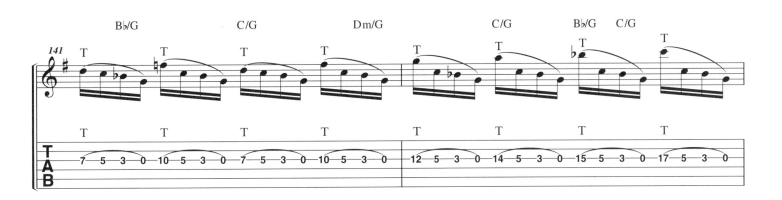

Fade out

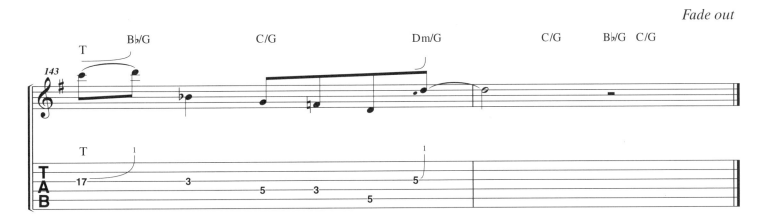

Rosanna - 10 - 10

ONLY WOMEN BLEED

Words and Music by
ALICE COOPER and DICK WAGNER

Only Women Bleed - 7 - 1

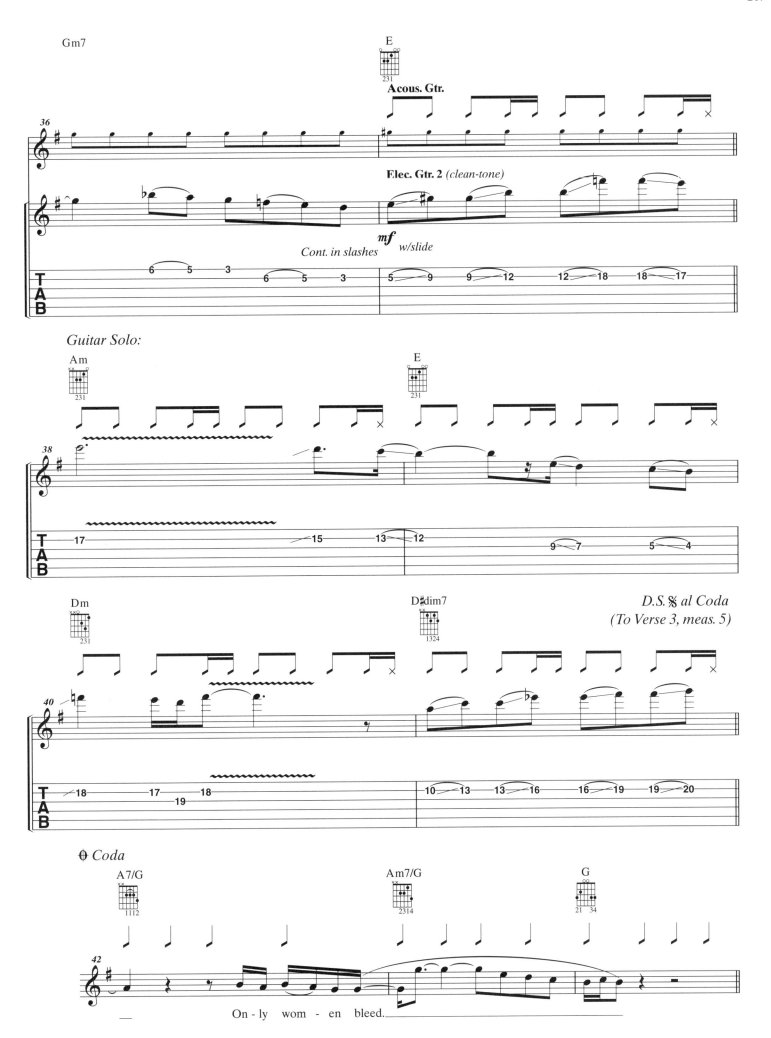

208

Instrumental:
Elec. Gtr. 1 tacet

Only Women Bleed - 7 - 6

SATURDAY IN THE PARK

Moderately ♩ = 120

Intro:

Words and Music by
ROBERT LAMM

Play 3 times

*Chord frames are for reference.
**Elec. Gtr. enters 2nd time.

Verse:

w/Rhy. Fig. 1 *(Elec. Gtr.) 2 times, simile*

1. Sat - ur - day___ in___ the park,___ I think it was the Fourth of Ju - ly.___
(2.) oth - er day___ in___ the park,___ I think it was the Fourth of Ju - ly.___ An -
3. Fun - ny days___ in___ the park;___ ev - 'ry day's the Fourth of Ju - ly.___

Sat - ur - day___ in___ the park,___ I think it was the Fourth of Ju - ly.___
oth - er day___ in___ the park,___ I think it was the Fourth of Ju - ly.___
Fun - ny days___ in___ the park,___ ev - 'ry day's the Fourth of Ju - ly.___

Peo - ple danc - ing, peo - ple laugh - ing, a man sell - ing ice___ cream,
Peo - ple talk - ing, real - ly smil - ing, a man play - ing gui - tar,
Peo - ple reach - ing, peo - ple touch - ing, a real cel - e - bra - tion

Saturday in the Park - 5 - 1

214

SMOKE FROM A DISTANT FIRE

Words and Music by
ED SANFORD, STEVEN STEWART
and JOHN TOWNSEND

Smoke from a Distant Fire - 8 - 1

half-time feel

Verse 1:

You left me here__ on your way__ to par - a - dise,__

you pulled the rug right out from un-der my__ life.__ I__ know__

end half-time feel

__ where you're go - in'__ to, I knew__ when you came__ home last__ night,__

Elec. Gtr. 1

220

Smoke from a Distant Fire - 8 - 5

Smoke from a Distant Fire - 8 - 8

(JUST LIKE) STARTING OVER

Words and Music by
JOHN LENNON

(Just Like) Starting Over - 10 - 1

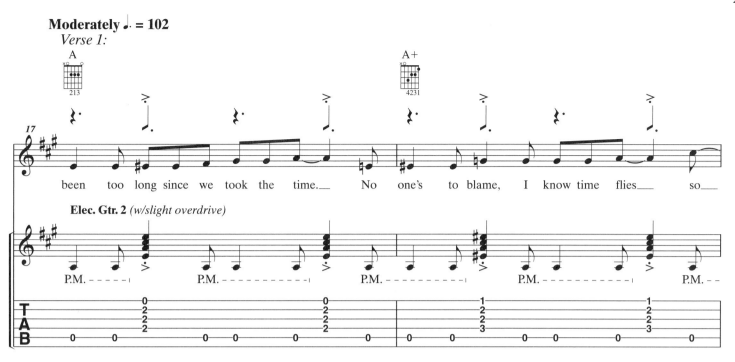

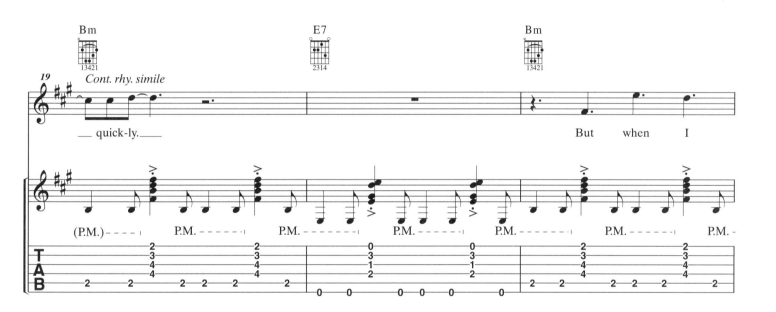

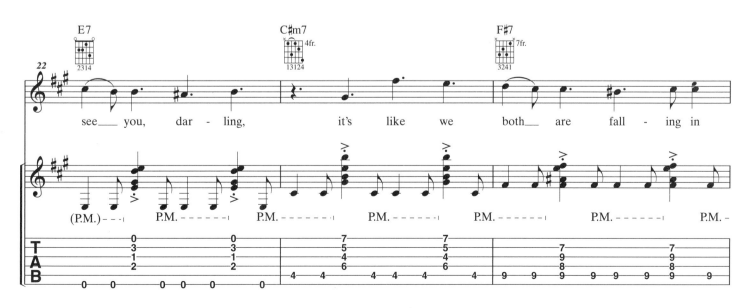

(Just Like) Starting Over - 10 - 2

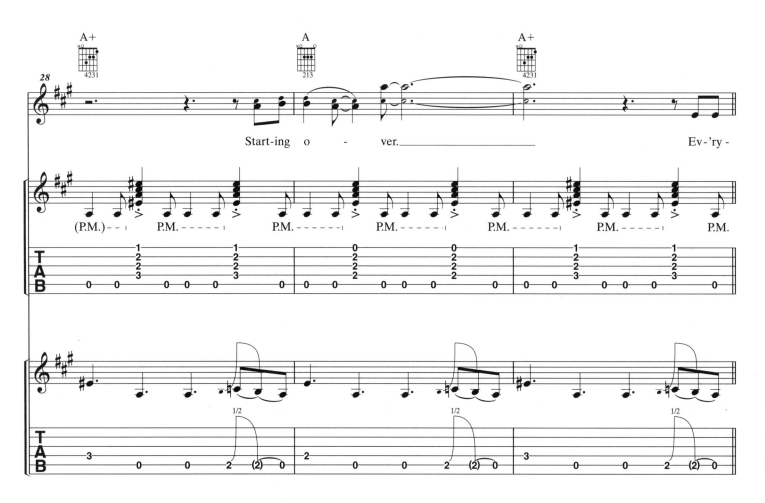

Verse 2:

day we used to make it, love,__ why__ can't we be mak-ing love__ nice____ and eas - y?

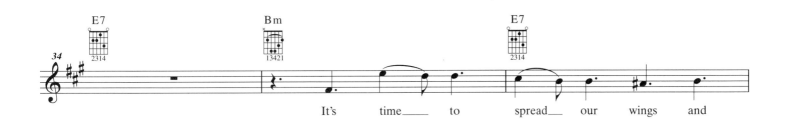

It's time____ to spread__ our wings and

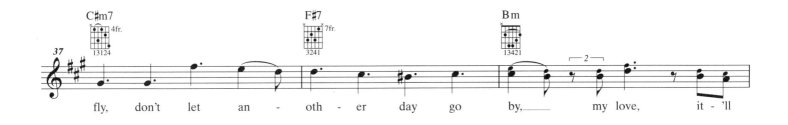

fly, don't let an - oth - er day go by,____ my love, it - 'll

be just like start - ing o - ver, start-ing

(Just Like) Starting Over - 10 - 4

(Just Like) Starting Over - 10 - 5

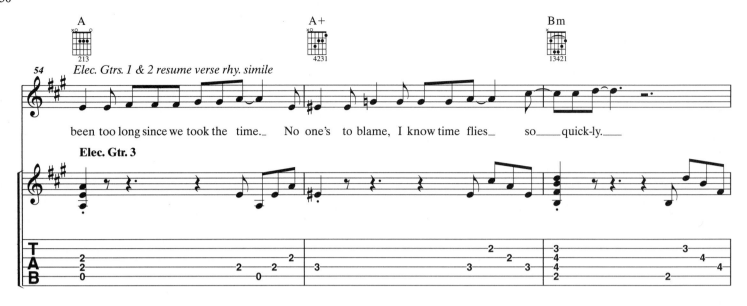

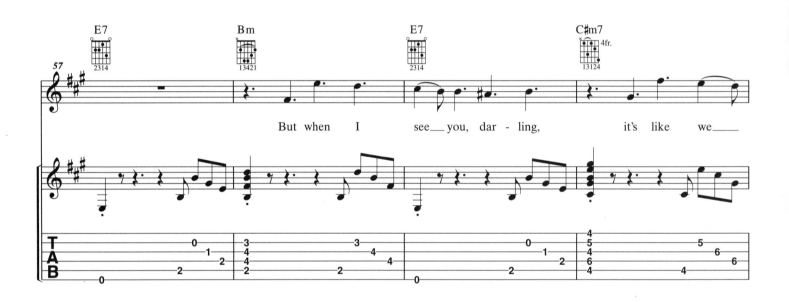

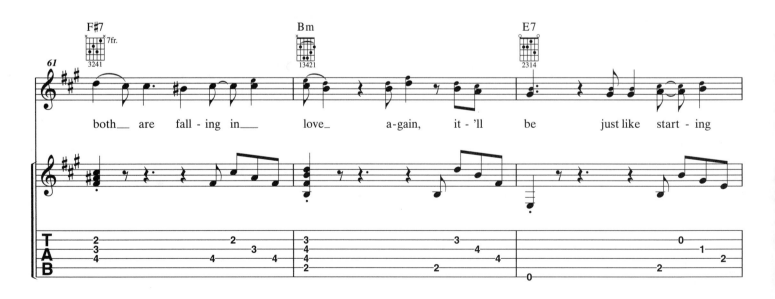

(Just Like) Starting Over - 10 - 8

(Just Like) Starting Over - 10 - 9

THIS MASQUERADE

Words and Music by
LEON RUSSELL

*Elec. Gtr. 2 dbld. by scat vocal.

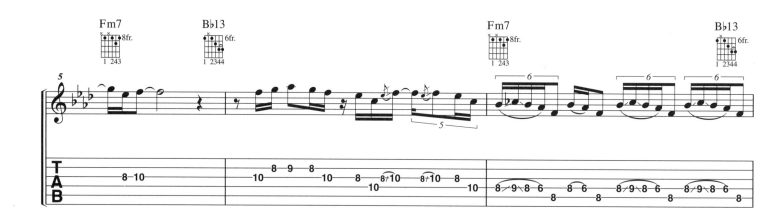

This Masquerade - 4 - 1

This Masquerade - 4 - 4

THUNDER ROAD

Words and Music by
BRUCE SPRINGSTEEN

Thunder Road - 6 - 1

Bridge:

Pre-chorus 2:

Thunder Road - 6 - 4

full of los-ers, I'm pull-ing out of here to win.

Outro:

Repeat and fade

Thunder Road - 6 - 6

TRUCKIN'

Words by ROBERT HUNTER
Music by JERRY GARCIA,
BOB WEIR and PHIL LESH

soft ma - chine,__ Hous - ton,__ too close to New Or - leans.__ New York __ got the
doo - dah__ man,__ once__ told me you got to play your__ hand.__ Some - times the cards ain't

ways an'__ means,__ but just won't let you be.__
worth a__ dime __ if you don't lay 'em down.__

w/Rhy. Fig. 1 *(Elec. Gtr.) 2 times,*
Chorus 2 only

Acous. Gtr.

*Elec. Gtr.

*Chorus 3 only, tacet on Chorus 2

Bridge:

Acous. Gtr. resume rhy. simile

Some - times__ the lights all shin - in' on me.__

Truckin' - 6 - 4

Verse 5:

You're sick of hang-in' a-round an' you'd like to trav - el.___ Get

tired of trav-el-in', you want to set-tle down.___ I guess they can't re-voke_ your soul for

D.S. % al Coda

try - in'.___ Get out of the door, light out and look all a - round.___

Elec. Gtr.

⊕ Coda   **Chorus 6:**

Truck-in',___ I'm_ a-go-in'_ home._ Whoa, whoa, ba-by, back where

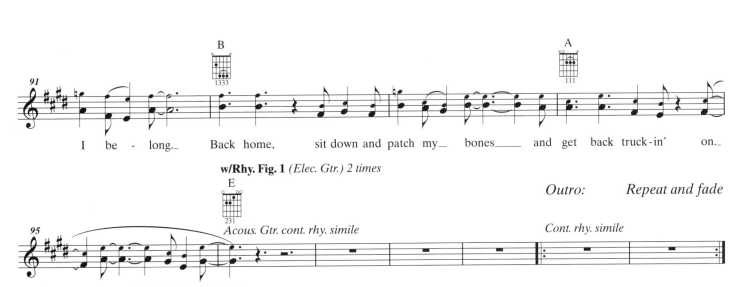

I be - long.___ Back home, sit down and patch my_ bones___ and get back truck-in' on._

w/Rhy. Fig. 1 *(Elec. Gtr.) 2 times*   *Outro:*   *Repeat and fade*

Truckin' - 6 - 6

WELCOME TO MY NIGHTMARE

Words and Music by
ALICE COOPER and DICK WAGNER

Moderately ♩ = 112

Intro:

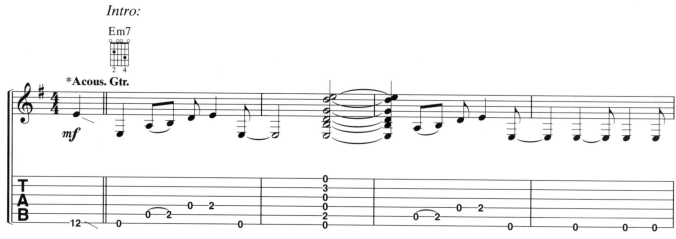

*Composite arrangement of two Acous. Gtrs. (6-string & 12-string).

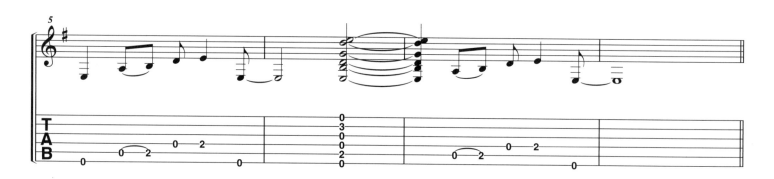

Verse 1:

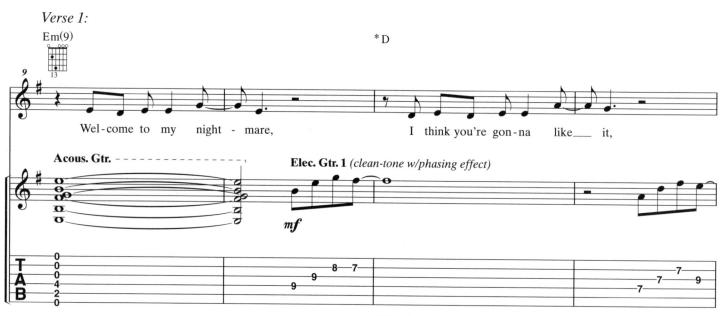

Wel-come to my night - mare,   I think you're gon-na like___ it,

*Chords are implied.

Welcome to My Nightmare - 6 - 1

*Chords are implied.

252

*Composite arrangement.

Welcome to My Nightmare - 6 - 3

Wel-come to my break-down!

Outro:

Yeah!

Welcome to My Nightmare - 6 - 6

WHAT A FOOL BELIEVES

Words and Music by
KENNY LOGGINS and MICHAEL McDONALD

*Chord frames throughout are for reference.

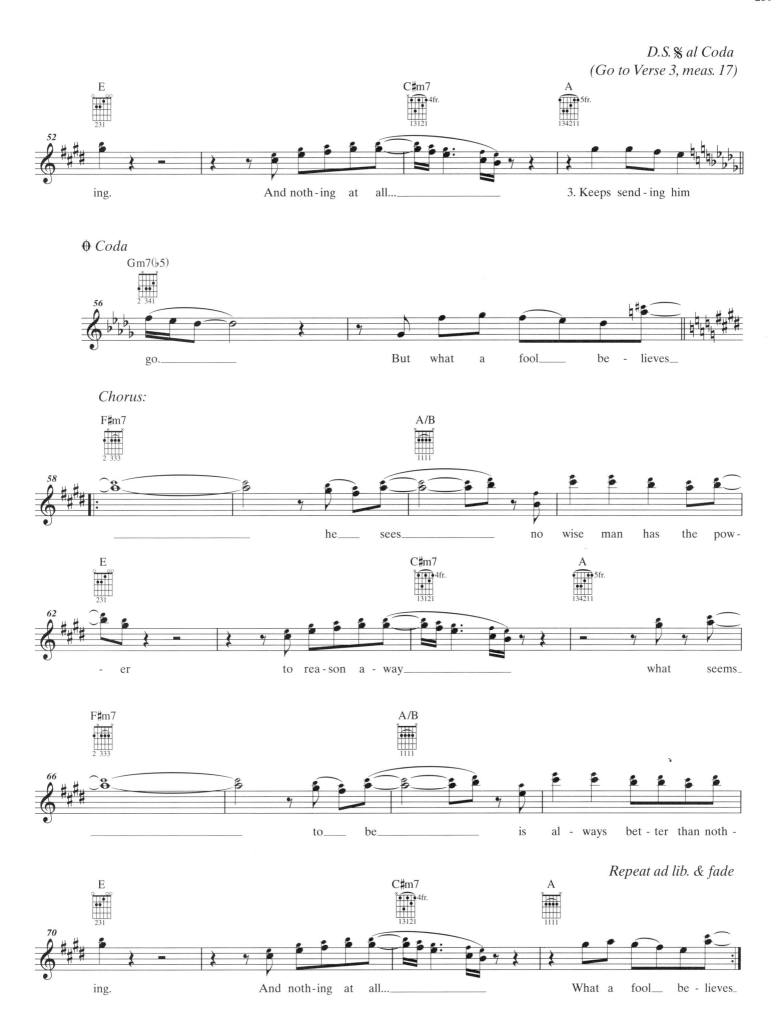

WHATEVER GETS YOU THRU THE NIGHT

Words and Music by
JOHN LENNON

Acous. Gtr. chord frames in concert key

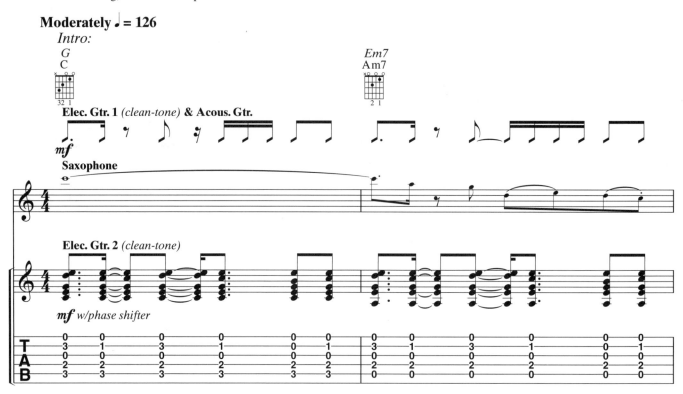

*To match recording, Elec. Gtrs. Capo VII

*Recording sounds a perfect fifth higher than written.

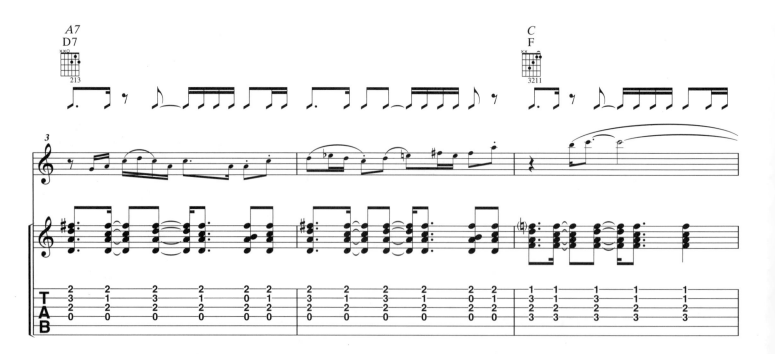

Whatever Gets You Thru the Night - 5 - 1